Wildflower Nation

Kaitlin Fleming

Also by Kaitlin Fleming

Butterfly Food

The Stars Are Free

Website: kaitlinfleming.com

Instagram: @kaitlnfleming

To Phil Stark,
an American hero

I've seen dark storms

give birth to wildflowers

New generations are coming,

One by one.

They will uncover secrets,

Discover promise,

And open the eyes

Of the world

To make it better.

If you had a second chance

You would be born again

But this time

Nothing

Would

Stop

You

What would you do for your country
With just a penny and a dime?
If your soul was kind
Your mind like wildfire
And compassion like steel
If your vision created gardens
And your hands were cupped open
Ready to drink from its streams

We're all lucky, we just have to figure out

What we're lucky about.

Every life is precious, exploring its own unique divinity.

We often get lost, forgetting our own humanity,

Who we are and where have we come from.

We are just fragmented pieces of the stars.

Let's sweep up the dust, determined to find out

Who we are so we can blossom into flowers to roam earth.

It's time to run wild and free,

Time to shovel out the bull that we tell ourselves,

Time to beckon a new sun and awaken like we are one.

Footsteps appear, we wait on the edge to find ourselves,

Looking to nature to guide us on our way,

Following the truth like a rainbow with a pot of gold.

But you are the currency, you are the imagination

That wells like a spring from a forgotten childhood.

There and everywhere, we find the answers,

Tie our shoes and open the lockets.

We aren't far removed, rather lurking in the darkness

That becomes so bright with golden tears.

Reap what you sow, continue to grow.

Reality is a canvas waiting for you to use your brush.

Don't turn away, you're alive to experience it all.

That is your gift.

You possess the power,

You hold the secret,

Beneath the edges

That embrace the

Forest's edge.

You sit with an unlit candle,

And it's your turn

To light the flame.

I counted the clouds

Until the rain decided to come.

The roses were withered pink,

And the ting of the bat brought us home.

Remember how we learned

To memorize everything?

That's all it was,

Because you can't teach passion.

No, that comes

From your innermost yearnings

That spark the feather

To take off and fly.

there is more fun in peace

than you will ever come to know

Your eyes were black holes,
Containing a thousand secrets.
I knew we'd be good friends.

The air is silent.

Nothing provokes it.

I'm down on my knees.

Do I celebrate

The deepness,

The empty space?

Can I find the melody

Somewhere as I stare

At my guitar?

Can life

Be this soothing?

Uncover the trauma from years ago

You're healing when you give it a voice

Past secret gardens

In the middle of the night

A rose bloomed

And you had no idea

If you could keep

It tucked inside

There would be

No glass to shatter

But the blooms

Made the glass break

In slow motion

It was cut open.

This time in the cold

Beauty b u r n s

Don't challenge me
You'll forget
What the challenge was
When I break it

Death is not an answer.

It's not an option,

Although you tried.

You had to fight

In long days spent

Amongst the hills,

Haunted.

You were made to live

With gold in your eyes.

We turned the car around

And went sailing down the road

To save the remnants

Before we faced the light

Without a filter

I can't heal you

When you are breaking me

Our personalities

Are beautiful gems

Designed for earth

Made for a purpose

Only the cosmos

Understand

It's an adding game.

How many good things

Can happen in one day?

Will you be a blessing for someone else?

Create an energy.

Make them feel alive.

We were born

Not to settle but to thrive.

Welcome to the city's vibe.

Cherish these rhythms; they get us by.

You've got one life, and the stars are high.

Reach them.

You were born cool

And you're going die cool

We can't always take each other in

Because the light is so precious

And we're afraid it will be gone

But let it glow

Feel the love

Even if it hurts

don't ask a pessimist for advice
they will tell you the wrong answer
every time

Shielded

By the

Forest

There was

A field

And a cabin

Bunnies

And doves

Broken cars

And dust

Lots of rust

Bolts

Railroad ties

Thorns

And a spring

From which

Only love

Flowed from

these roads are rough

just ask the turtle on the highway

You don't need to look back
at where you came from
You just need to know
who you are now
Windows half shut
I open it full swing
let the light come in
Happiness feels good again

you found potential in me
even with pizza on my face

On the edge of the precipice

Hanging on

Before the light becomes dim

Will I awaken

Like tulips of spring?

Push back across the

Cold shore?

Can I create

A magic destiny

To outlast time's

Hand on me?

Through the blinds,

The sun sparkles

On the green

And red leaves,

And it says, "Child, you'll be okay."

Make life precious to you.

Bend down, pick the wildflowers,

Follow the sun.

Phone less.

People more.

Your light could be the light that leads someone home.

It could inspire a painter to use their brush,

Influence the writer to pick up their pen,

Bring someone to the stage to act.

Open doors, hold visions,

Help a stranger, craft a smile,

Endure the coldest night for a cup of tea,

Open the flower most ready to bloom.

Yes, light gives your spirit a lift,

And when it does, ride it.

Give it away, accept it, free it, store it, hold it.

Your light is a secret no one knows

Where it came from, how you got it,

Or where it's going to go.

Sometimes it is peace that comes over us,

Our hearts frozen then thawed, weak and then brave.

Broken hearts survive by placing light inside the cracks.

Heat molds and bends things into solid form,

A welder who wields the flame,

Sees the butterfly on the coldest of days.

Our peace is our universe, all roads lead to one.

Fly butterfly fly,

Grab your torch, fix your heart.

And let peace be your art.

I am happiest when I remember who I am.

I need lows

Like I need highs,

Fill me up like mud

In between stones.

Green grasses grow

At their brightest level.

I thought my country failed me,

Then I turned around.

you have a mind of your own

when you turn the light on

you won't be afraid

On the bank

In the sunshine

We decided

We would give up

Our lives for you that day

But life doesn't work that way

Yearning to be understood

Like you got dropped off in the desert

Walking towards tomorrow

Holding a letter only the sun can read

Technology is the new water

Nourishing growth

Fueling innovation

Fostering beauty

But only when it serves a purpose

And ignites our imagination

Uncover the brilliance of your soul
It was meant to glow like sunlight on snow.

We are given choices

As if they are seeds

We hold them

Plant them

Pray for them

And watch them thrive

It's on calm nights

I feel sad

Because I know

There's a storm

Coming.

It's a miracle

We go through this life

With each other,

Braving the days

That we go without.

If you watch a flame

It will breathe

It will flicker

It will burn

But you watching

Makes all the difference

the mind craves challenges

they give us a reason

to be here

I'll float, fly, and soar,

But in it, I know there's more,

Like these wings could lift up a ceiling,

Pull a house up from its foundation,

Move this world made of angel dust.

The darkness feels heavy on our lids.

To be good is to be defined by action.

We seek wisdom in the middle of the day.

We grieve, but summon the courage to open the door

And say "let's explore".

We move the lanterns across the floor,

Shove the book under the door;

This is your process, this is your beginning.

If I light the way, you're coming with me.

I won't let you drown because the stars don't wait;

They walk down a million roads just to say hello.

There was a gateway

And you walked through it

Old and new at the same time

You were changed forever

The sound of wet streets
competes with the music
Lights are reflecting
fluorescent and shiny
I come alive again and again

You woke up

at just the right time

to do something

But how would that set you free?

Open the windows,

Stare down the halls.

Time is your quest,

When all that blossoms

Moves through your fingertips.

The world is better on a bike.

Can I keep up with the latest technology?
Is this world leaving me in the dust
with nothing but poetry?
Is that enough?

We are dutiful
like spring rain

Not only do you have the power

To change this country

But to keep it special

And make it come alive

Goth kid left me in the dust.
I think I can watch this town
In my rainbow shirt.

Bring me a society

That allows humans

To be as free as willow trees

The mind is ever active,

It never fades away.

You can unlock it

Like a treasure chest,

And discover the jewels

That have been there

From the very start.

The universe wants you
to make a difference on this planet
and you'll do it, the only way you know how
Sometimes you're wearing bright shoes
sometimes you're taking in the view
or wearing a backwards hat
But once in a while you're listening
really listening and that frees someone
Like you opened a cage for a bird
Put the last piece on the puzzle
Dreamed bigger than anyone had
and it saved the world

Rose gold

I am sold

Innuendos knock on my door

I leave roses

Searching for the light

I see it

More clear

Than diamonds

Kaitlin Fleming

You need to find peace
Where you left her,
By a cherry blossom
Under a blue sky.

If it wasn't powerful,

It wouldn't have

Been given to you.

Dice it out,

Find the stalemate.

Trust in truth,

Surrender purpose

Like leaves falling.

You're on the edge

Of time,

Looking into

The abyss.

Some people are therapy.

You're on a roller coaster;

It is your life.

Strive to be happy,

Because it'll be over,

And you'll ask,

"What was the point?"

I saw a monk

With an electric guitar

See how far the stars

Really open the mind

How our songs do rhyme

Sifting in the shadows

We wait to bloom

Uncover our tombs

Or vanish into clouds up high

A genius has the capacity
To change the world,
But if they are hungry,
They can't achieve.
If they are void of love,
They will not want to.
If they think little of themselves,
They will remain hidden.
But when a genius is fulfilled,
Watch them become a storm
With lightning striking
From their mind.

It's a hard world. Be as soft as a pansy petal.

You can wear many hats,

But usually, there's

One chosen for you.

In the fault lines, shadows dance gracefully,
Revealing patterns to discern the voice of God.
Leading me down corridors to a better life,
Where fate awaits to be seen.

When you are present

You have access

To this dimension

And it looks a lot

Like steam rising

From my tea

I'm going to the city with a different attitude.

We were made to be beautiful.

Why would we want it

Any other way?

United we stand,

Searching for the essence.

Maybe we can catch it.

I got butterflies on my desk

Something beautiful in my chest

A heart that

Beats like wings

Meant to fly

Come to my bookshelf

You'll see no fiction

Only reality and

How we've come to change it

sometimes I live so close to the edge
that I feel like I'm not coming back

There is a garden of things I want to learn.

If I listen, enchanted by drums in the street,

Worms in their holes, church bells echoing,

Time is growing towards a mass unaccounted for.

I want to know these things.

I want to hunt down the dust,

The ivory, the sacred stones, the pebbles,

Touch them, and know them for the first time,

Like looking at glass.

I want to know the reflection,

The peace in every neighborhood,

Even if it's big or small.

I want to feel the breeze over flower boxes,

Smell the creek, reflect on the leaves.

I want to be time and let everything float through me,

Because if I don't, then I shall cry,

Because life would pass me by,

And I want to live it like no other.

They say you are oblivious,

But do they know

You pay attention to what matters?

Some days I want to be a hermit

And never come back.

Sometimes I want to be a rock star

And never come down.

Kaitlin Fleming

He had a green hat

With an American flag on it

He was gold

If you have a strong inner world
life is a lot easier on the outside

Ode to the imagination

Dreams happen in the strangest of ways

Leave a path as bright as a constellation

Abandon the purpose

But find it hidden in time

From a light nobody knows

The world swallows night

And closes the light

But gets up to do it again

This life is art,

And we treat it like wallpaper.

Homes have sculptures, paintings,

And spider plants.

I want to go down spiral staircases

And find myself in the basement,

Make a garden,

Bring it up under skylights.

Who knew we could grow fruits

Inside our heads?

Let the world come alive

So we can find everything

We need to understand.

Kaitlin Fleming

A sip of coffee

And my dreams return

80

I vow to take care of myself

even if the system does not let me

I kneel down

periwinkle surrounds me

in the groundcover of this land

I trust that the light leads the way

to embody a spiritual life

even in the chaos

I am brave

I embrace my truth

I know

We both

Lay awake crying

Because

We

Are

Twins

Your intuition

Will break

Into what is hidden

And you'll find yourself

Listening

Vulnerable

To the voice of God

Break open

The sound of love

It's just music

Telling you

That you have always been home

We must have full acceptance

Of what we are

To overcome the hurdles

We hold within

under the mess of it all

is a realm of artistic perfection

So committed to yourself

You flew across the country

And never looked back

That was the best decision

You ever made

We've become so disconnected

That we don't remember

What it's like

To be connected

Like a bird
Eating a worm,
Let our bellies
Be full of life.

Sit on the mountain top

Sing a song

Of resilience

Echoing

The high peaks

To deliver

A sonnet

That embarks

On the discovery of a new world

Where gold lies

This is a sacred life.

You are tired,

Like wagon wheels,

Pure like the dust they roll through.

But you've come across the fields to fly.

Now, on this earth, nothing is a lie.

Everything is what it's worth.

Feel a rose,

Feel a stone,

Come alive.

Art is there when you need it
To pierce through the clouds
Or to illuminate the sun
When it's already shining

You're getting your joy back,
And nothing can break its path.

Bring truth to the top

Open the mind

And find zeros inside

We are going to split the atom

Move coal until the rails are spinning

Over the fields

Wildflowers pass us by

We are so lucky

You should stay where you shine.

Yearning for clouds

To read our minds

A new direction

Isn't hard to find

We hold steady

For the gold

Shoot from the coal

Let the love soar

This time

We achieve epiphanies

Where we left them

At the front door

Clear the forest floor

Change sweeps the streams

Life awaits

Every aching step

In every new moment

We're like ducks

Floating down the creek

Bumping into rocks

September skies open

Happiness is a space

Move in

Buy the furniture

And live

Some people have a look in their eye as if they have bigger dreams. I admire that.

You keep hitting a brick wall
but you are not broken

Did darkness really need to come

and take us?

Could we be dancing in the light

before it fades us?

Not sure why I'm a victim

when I'm just here for the ride.

Celebrate truth through the underpass;

I've laid roots

and they don't laugh.

Time to hold the candlestick,

watch the flame hit the sun.

It might rain,

but watch the peonies grow.

People make mistakes,

but hunny, I assure you,

clouds don't.

So let it fly,

let it rain,

let it burn.

Time's creating a melody for you.

truth doesn't need words

it needs silence to carry it

Kaitlin Fleming

Each person is rare

Come to know them deeply

Save your mind

Maybe it

Will save the world

Don't move the wand if you can't handle the magic.

There's a god behind everything

Directing you which way to go

Take it slow

Listen for the whisper

It wants to deliver

Never looking for the chance

But it comes to you

Through this breath of life

That only the jet stream can hold onto

Jigsaw puzzle around this life

It's up and down

Carry it holy with rhythm

So you can dance among its tracks

Like rivers flow, so as time it goes

But embedded are the acts of love

Of which beneath needs no framework to function

I smile 'cause you

Don't know what I'm up to

Starving for safety

I wrap my arms

Around loneliness

To embrace the fact

That I'm just a piece of matter

Held in place by gravity

Despondent to the ocean's tides

Held by the moon

When will I collide

Like snowflakes on a windy day?

When do I dare?

Has your love note fallen to the ground?

To be tortured in the dirt before it was found?

Are the stars free,

Or did they have to work?

Did they have to bleed?

What's the secret?

Our unhappiness

Peaks like a mountain.

Why can't we get to the source of it?

I took firecrackers

Let them explode

Watched as they wove into midnight dreams

Into satin mysteries

That left the world questioning

Kaitlin Fleming

our mission

tastes like blackberries

faded by the sun

He raises himself up to the sky

To fix the electric line,

So we can see at night.

Does he know that he is the light?

Your soul came back

When you scratched off the surface

And blew the dust away

The day we bought the paintings,

I let my demons go,

And let love reside.

Without my eyeliner,

I looked more real.

I lifted up my sunglasses

Because I wanted

To see the people shine

Junk food stars,

Polish yourself

So you can shine.

Wispy days

Scream "hooray,"

But all you want

Is a buttercup chin,

Kind of soul.

I am not a warrior

Nor am I a hero

I am but a delicate cosmos

Hold me up to the sky

You are perfect.

Don't be afraid of the shadows

They are caused by light

The time is now

You are here to live

And see the little things

The city moves with a velocity
The trees move with philosophy

You want anything and everything all at once,

But you can only have what the universe

Keeps stored inside.

Sometimes that means waiting,

Sometimes that means going numb,

Sometimes that means feeling the rush

Of a river flow through you

Until you've reached the other side.

And you know the universe

Is alive, working with you,

Forgetting time as an actual event,

But as a love that bends.

It's up to you to see the circus,

The crystal ball,

The highlight.

It's up to you

To know the vision,

The secret,

The core.

It's up to you to thirst for more,

Making your garden

As beautiful as you want.

I wilt like a rose,

Frozen in time,

Waiting for spring rain

To break the day.

This fate covers no lies.

When I feel the ground,

I will kiss it.

We are descendants of the night
born to make this road bright

You have been given

This small time slot in history to love

And watch the human heart begin to fly

If you want me to breathe

Realize robots don't

The sun can't shine

Cause we were born

With blood

Connected to our hearts

Broken

In this world,

But we can heal.

Use Maslow as a map,

Open the attic door,

Let the light in.

Success is living life deeply.

Before you get too old
Take a spiritual journey
Across this country
Make it for you

Bring forth

The beauty in a field

Ready to ignite

A rainbow's truth

Spilled over the edge

To collect the ice

I'm not afraid

To let the light in

Give me fireworks

I want the sky to explode

Look around

You are a tree

An island

A star

A vision

Don't let anybody steal your pride

Steal your soul

Seal your life

There are some who prove

The human heart

Can never grow old

Joy is an acceptance

And a practice

Brave men

Go into the storm

And make it disappear

The secrets of those

Who've gone before us spread thin.

Your arms, they wrap me from within.

Brave new world, let's begin.

I've seen you, where have you been?

Winding down across town,

There's a million pieces.

Grab yours, little girl,

You've been on a wild ride.

You've had patience inside.

Now blow dust that becomes

A sky full of butterflies.

Don't tell me how to feel,

You'd have to know the universe inside me first.

You've got the traffic all figured out,

But you lost the stars long ago.

Let the train take you back,

Or get on a bike.

Take the trails marked in rustic gold.

Under the moon, you'll be still.

This time, your presence is like a dove.

Before you do anything ask,
"Is this healthy for me?"

Let it eat you alive,

Or you can face it.

I want you to keep unfolding me,

Get to the bones of me.

Realize we're

Made of the same stuff.

You will find the sun

Touch it like a god

Burn off the night

And bloom into day

Like you were being born

Kaitlin Fleming

When you stopped

Sending me your love,

I ripped

The plug out

And put the lamp

In the attic.

When your head is down

When your eyes are searching

When your feet are walking

When your heart is pumping

Remember to be happy

Kaitlin Fleming

Bruised self on the floor

I will help you get up

You grew up poor

But you didn't talk about it

Because your hearts

We're so rich

Having boundaries

Makes people nervous

Like you're protecting

Something they don't have

That feeling when you get out of school.

Anxiety catches my bones

Makes the wind feel like ice

Beneath my voice

Frozen, paralyzed by a fate untrue

God has given me fruit

I will eat

Find strength

Be renewed

Walk this land with faith

And nothing else

Skating on ice

That melts into water

And swims through my body

You can't take me down

I've got a river for a soul

And it moves into the depths

Of the countryside

Where a peaceful life resides.

I met a prophet on my coffee break

He said we will grow and bloom

If I get quiet

That's when you know

I'm feeling something

He said, "Godspeed," and she felt relieved,

Hope brings tremendous things.

You move on, ready to go,

Time to show the world what you know,

Because time is going to bring fabulous things.

Watch changes occur and see the wind

Blow destiny open, gates that were closed.

Walkway, there's time in faith and faith in time.

Kaitlin Fleming

We all turn brave
When we hear the anthem.

Jet stream,

You wake the blood stream

There are no rules

Except the ones we carve from our heart

Fly

Undetected

All we can ask

Is to help

In the evolution of each other

Providing basic needs

Love, and self-esteem

So we can fly

Like shooting stars

When we are ready

Kaitlin Fleming

You have a team of people

That lift you up

Thank them every day

You've been trying to sound like them
But all the while, your sound
Was that of a flame flickering in night
Challenged by naked air
That would bellow out
And offer the tiniest bit of hope
Maybe that's all you need

There is no soul in this city

It is give and take

Diamonds and cars

Bright signs and plastic scars

The soul is coerced

Solid, not coming back

It flew away on its own

To surrender in the dark

You must be the gardener

Of your soul

The work is hard

But when the dawn comes

You will see the beauty of the blooms

Because peace prevails in the soil you moved

The spirit you watered

The mess you replanted

You stayed true

To glitter in the sidewalks

The stamp that said freedom

You may be tired now

But feel your spirit revive

Watch the dust clear out and fly

There's so much to live for

Touch heaven

With the faith of a feather

Blow the dandelion

Until all the seeds come out

You will be what you imagine

It's Friday

I'm wearing a polo

And a hoodie

Listening to The Killers

Outside

The sun shines

Just another badge

No matter where I go

I will always be a nomad

Diseased by a bug

all the other trees die too

Lift up the light

in the night

through the fog

You might be

the last hope in sight

but you're going to fight

until the trees die

and marigolds

wake the fields

You will live a fabulous life

Because you will live it on your terms

And that, my friend

Will serve the masses

He said nothing is

Free in this country

It takes work

And forgiveness

Love and meditation

To bring opportunity

And open eyes

To this life

As it floats by

There are chills in your body

Symphonies in your mind

Take the keys and find

Epiphanies

Where truth lies

Willing to take a stand

My hope for you is to open

The locket and see yourself

And the goodness

That you are

The brightness that you shed

The rain that you drink

Before your trip home

One day I just let it all go

The good, the bad, the ugly

I picked up a torch

And carried it as if walking through darkness

Could be fun

But when the break of dawn came

I put it down

Because a torch isn't needed under the sun

when four eyes lock

they say a thousand words

Kaitlin Fleming

Be more present with yourself
So you can be more present with other people.

You can't run

Shattered glass

Smoke and ash

You're born with a flag

Tied up and broken

You're unspoken until you unfold your wings

And become the lotus

His soul was a tiny sailboat

Creating ripples

Which turned to waves

And made all the difference

Nothing's off the table

You can be as brave

And as rare as you want

They will talk about the trauma that hit you,

But they can't talk about the explosion of light

That deepened your every experience and made it sparkle.

Let the silence

Shake you to your core.

Let it crawl into your bones.

Let it stop at nothing.

Let it draw blood from your beating heart.

Let it swallow the air.

This, my friend,

Is absorbing.

This, my friend, is treating the presence

With a passion.

And when you are done

Holding it fiercely,

Let go of the moment.

You will have something to say.

We are just skin and bones borrowing from the Earth.

the candle is lit

we only blow it out

because we are going places

The days were long, but when night came,

There was a thin line of pink

Skimming the sky.

Travel life, figure out the whys.

When we see a cop

We all slow to the same speed

One nation with many stars

I think we need to believe

That we were born to kiss the ground

And let our legends fly free

I heard your soul

Singing to me

Through the radio

So I turned it up

Don't forget

Your pain

Is a marker

A clue

For what's in store for you

Like a key

That unlocks the door

Bright colors

Will show

Their path

And you

Will move along

Never

Tasting

The vibrancy

Without

The rain

Kaitlin Fleming

This time I'm going with you

Racing you

The train on the tracks

From all the love you ever showed me

I'm with you

On this ride

Hand out the window

Waving because

We are not alone

We've seen people go

To the moon and back

The world is at your fingertips

Kaitlin Fleming

You didn't think it could hurt to be the sun

But when the clouds roll by

You realize otherwise

sometimes it takes

perfect chemistry

for the soul to grow

The sun broke down upon me

The rays stretching out to earth

Whispering the secrets

Of God's worth

Nothing but tears rain down

Holy is the ground

Holy are the steps we take

Holy are the words we breathe

Holy is the ladder

That we climb from earth into the sky

This is the real money.

At the end of the day

I empty my purse.

What did I have to collect?

Oh, did I collect a smile

That created laughter?

This is the money that we need.

This city hasn't changed,

You just grew wings

To see it from above.

You walk the extra mile for people

Maybe one day

Someone will run

A marathon for you

Born of great creators

We revel in the philosophy

Of our ancestors

But carry on

With a new version of ourselves

Tormented by not knowing self

We float away

Kaitlin Fleming

I'll make light

In the basement

And leave the windows upstairs

For you

In bright algae on the pond

The opening of clouds

The bird who sings its song

The chills on windy walks

The purple in the thorns

The smile you cracked

The wisdom you wore in that hat

The smell of smoke in the distance

The sound of a distant bat

What she said

He said

Boiling it down

To make a certain sound

In your head

Above the grasses that sit

Calm in the dark

Crickets and frogs chirp

Under a sky full of stars

What a wonderful life

Your childhood is a soundtrack
As if preserved in a museum
Like it was something classic

plant wildflowers on the moon

and tell me what it looks like

I'm here for peace

And peace only

Don't ask me

To be something different

Life gets busy

And you work on improving

Your career

Your hobbies

Your home

But beneath the clutter and the mess

You forget to work on improving yourself

Because you aren't any of those things

You are the flame on the candle

And it needs your attention

I'll fly on nothing but a tiny fire inside.

you're a morning glory

you'll grow

where it is unthinkable

This land wanted you to see hope

And know it as a friend

This time, you're going to look

At the ground and realize

This is your last trip around

Dance like a leaf

Making the most of its time

Before the bright colors fade.

You feel the water

Dripping down your windows

On the highway

You move like a dove

Finding peace

Is like

Feeling

Love

This is only the beginning

Your journey will take you a lot further

If you let it

Just like that, she took back her power

With the slide of a button

Brand new

Like shoes

With new laces

Smarter

Kinder

Braver

Kaitlin Fleming

It's a full moon, watch wolves roam,

Time to sing and time to show.

You will win a thousand highs,

Touch the diamond skies.

Born so great that you could fly,

Never will your spirit die.

The winter will come like thunder,

And you will move under

The ocean's heavy waves,

To quest the depth

Of secret caves.

Without doubt, you will find

The truth of your mind.

Some days you are on top of the world,

And some days you are beneath it, feeling the weight.

In the morning,

I opened the blinds

And there was a hummingbird

On the hibiscus

Tasting each flower

We are social creatures

Born to talk

Not judge photos

Bring about

The version of ourselves

To download

And press the play button

That is our

Dance floor

The possibility

Of adding to the music

My friends start revolutions.

We will plant impatiens

In stone boxes

March inside

Sacred places

With our minds budding

Are you related to the

Wonders of this universe?

Find a fine grain of wheat

Hold it in your hand

There is magic

There is life

Cut open raw sores

That lead to insight

Pick the lavender

You will smell the essence

Breathing love into the air

Happiness feels real on this planet

See the people

Imagine their stories

See their smiles

Soak it up like the sun

I believe this ice will melt

And we can all be as one

We often strive

To make our lives comfortable

But when do we fully commit

To pursuing our true passions?

You won't halt

At the mural's edge

Letting waves crash down

Everything you've found

Reduced to paper ashes

For the fire has its own sound

Like life does

In the dead of night

When you tear a page from the book

Simple lives

Simple dreams

Simple hopes

The grasses don't cry

They grow

They become green

They give us a place to lay our head

Our souls may be buried under bad decisions

But we can grab the shovels

Under a moonlit sky

And dig ourselves up

When the world feels so big

That's when our hearts

Are most open

I was eating popcorn

Like I was eating life

Jamming it down my throat

Life is better with community.

In this valley, we can be a ton of things
And one of them is magic

When the light becomes so bright,

And it washes over you in waves,

Remember this one thing:

You were made for this.

You are the picture on the wall

The piano notes sifting through the air

The tea kettle making steam

You are the little things that circle round

Like images in your dreams

You are a blank slate, ready to take place

Trace memories and make them gold

Find tough times and make them

Precious gems for the soul

You're the rainbow at the end

Chanting the runner to cross the line

You're the passerby waiting for a friendly smile

To light the way

Don't back down today

You have potential

Through the darkness was a beautiful light

Caged birds were freed

Red turned to green

Clouds rolled by as you wondered why

You got a chance to be anything at all

I walk away from negativity

Because it does not feed my soul.

I see light in the dark,

And I have won.

Surviving is what

I've done.

Kaitlin Fleming

You have all the courage in the world

Underneath mountains

Through tunnels

Voyaging through time

You will find a way to use it

Home of the free

Born of the brave

Watching clocks like raindrops

Look at what blooms beneath the surface

A light unclaimed

Reunited at last

In the lights and in the sounds

I want to cry

Pull it all down

This life is strangely painful

Yet beautiful

And we just make it what we want it to be

Your heart creates new patterns

That the universe will understand.

Watch your leap of faith

Fall off a dusty cliff.

The place wasn't alive until you got here.

Courage isn't easy,

But who said it would be anyway?

Gravitate to the light, find insight,

Across concrete, into the holes

That fell through the cracks,

Inside the mind where flowers grow wild

Through the grass.

In times like these, hearts may hurt,

But they also hunger,

Hunger for adventure and truth,

Hunger to find someone alive in the madness,

Courageous and bold enough to lead the way.

Light is felt when we lean in

To serendipitous beginnings.

Your imagination grows like fountains,

Ready to express the story of wind and dust,

Capturing soul for a moment

Only to be traced in particles aligned with music

That will never be forbidden.

Let it carve out your soul

And create a mosaic of dreams

That you run and leap into.

You are an individual

With one destiny

And limitless potential

Let the wind and the rain

Heal your pain

For nature's touch

Works wonders every time

Darkness holds tight the quest

To embark on journeys

That take us further than we can see.

Stop, hold your breath.

You are a part of the universe

That has a song for you

In motion

Beneath the stars

To embody the leaves

That are like tokens on the trees.

You can love something

And yet it may not be right for you

You can grow sideways

And upside down

And see truth

As it is in stairwells

Timeless and uninterrupted

Simple, yet forgiving

Whimsical, like satin

You are the dream

Nothing changes

It ebbs and flows

But there's a line

Like fire

That opens wisdom

Beneath the ground

And hunts you down

You may be lost, child

But one day you will be found

Take a sick day

Remember your dreams

Your smile's back
The world can see

Forgotten forest, where do we roam?

Inside truth, there is a stone,

Sifting through the stars at night,

Bring me back to twilight,

Where we see a world unknown,

Before wisdom took the throne.

Wisest wish moves with ease,

Sometimes the soul is the only thing to please.

I spent an hour watching Blue Jays

Out the window

With my puppy

That was time spent well

Gold angels loom

Holding whispers in the wind

Grasses flowing

The world below races

But you are steady

Because you are the sky

We take this life

And deem to make it true.

Our responsibility

Is to make it sacred

So we can know meaning

In empty windows

And soar as high as an eagle.

Brave enough to know the nature of the sun,

Carry us epiphanies.

Challenge the myths so we can

Know of a love

So alive.

Love in the spring

Joy in the summer

But your heart

It beats all seasons

To ignite

Truth and its reasons

Brush your fingers through the meadows

Find strength inside

Something about this life that screams love

Across the lakes to the shore

Find forests that awaken gardens

That unlock secret souls

Twisted and broken, we can see life will open

To mirrors and hopes

Ferns have patterns like our hearts have their purpose

Meditate, find yourself in the essence

Nurturing self with nature, we grow

We take quests to hunt down the truth inside

Offer wisdom wherever you go

There are many signs

You'll know when your light is needed

The darkness will separate

America, your trees are bare
But look at the growing leaves
The ones that dare
Search for lighthouses on the shore
Don't lose sight of the vision
That was fought for

Watch wetlands turn into meadows
See mountains skim the sky
Always try, never give up
The words of the stars
Were written and sometimes mistaken for scars

But behind the curtain of time
Forgiveness is the start
Be brave like butterflies
And become bold like fireflies
Carrying light into the dark

It's the hum of the lawn mower

The bent-over tiger lilies

Each unique blade of grass

The chirping of birds at dusk

It's the light that carries us through

Bringing us to the next dawn

If only we're in the moment

In the end, you realize the world is a family,
And you'd do anything for it.

Eyes stare straight at you

The moment isn't seized

Drift remains unclosed

Life's unfolding

Have you sharpened your tools?

Allow time a chance to stir

Your feet move beneath the sea

Wind propels grass to new heights

Born before, hurdling arrows toward future dreams

That cannot wait

Let the roses be crushed by the weight

Of a thousand freight trains

I see no other way

underneath attraction

look for soul

I've felt calm winters

And smiles as warm as summer

Frost sparkling outside my window

Sunsets pink as hell

I see you everywhere

And though

I tend to forget

I have you

I hold you

In between

The sunshine and the clouds

The street

It haunts the blood inside

We move with a beat

Unified

Breathe

This city has a love so rare

Watch the lights change

This is your courage

And it's green, this is the scene

Open your soul

The wind will blow you south side

You will live because baby you're alive

Move through the door

This city is dirty

But it's filled with truth of every kind

There is no divide because the minds collide

And we reach out like stars

Dreaming awake in our beds, tucked in

This city doesn't sleep because there's a new dawn

And it makes it more awake than it's ever been

Kneel down now and believe in its brilliance

Dark clouds hover
On the horizon
But you walked in
And it kicked in
Human hearts
Create the mood

If we had a little more grace

Towards each other

That would be a gentle thing

Perhaps it would light a spark

Set fire to the land

And make wildflowers grow

You take risks in this world

For just a bit of sunshine

Wherever you go

Whatever you see

Don't lose that

Kaitlin Fleming

Read words that light your mind

Here you wake

Haunted, but revived

Alive and stretching truth to its fullest potential

You'll find vision through your tracks

Pushing daisies into hot sunny afternoons

Where you find the wind moves your hair

Follow that epiphany through

The sun doesn't shine

It was buried, but brought up

So you can see the light of your soul ignite

Prove yourself

Only time can tell

What you're worth

But I see pennies

That mean nothing

But good luck

Send a sunflower

Into an open pocket

The ghost of old meanings

You're striking life

Like lightning

Ready to hatch open symphonies

Lost in blades of grass

Kneel down

Touch the fire

Face the spirit

In nature

Bring it home

So you can find words.

The relationship you have with yourself

Is one you will never end

Nourish it

I'm happy to see

The sparkles in the waves

At the lake on a sunny day

Souls do that too

They sparkle

Without knowing their course

Or how they affect each other

But when the sky is blue after fire

We can begin anew

Calling our actions art

Fighting another day

To delve into self

And pull something out

This time

Don't be afraid

To sparkle

Remember to wake me

When I'm caught sleeping

Naps are quick

But this is life

This is it

www.ingramcontent.com/pod-product-compliance
Lightning Source LLC
LaVergne TN
LVHW041212080426
835508LV00011B/929